Look for other

titles:
World's Weirdest Critters
Creepy Stuff
Odd-inary People
Amazing Escapes
World's Weirdest Gadgets
Bizarre Bugs
Blasts from the Past

Awesome Animals

by Mary Packard

and the Editors of Ripley Entertainment Inc.

illustrations by Leanne Franson

SCHOLASTIC INC.

New York   Toronto   London   Auckland   Sydney
Mexico City   New Delhi   Hong Kong   Buenos Aires

Developed by Nancy Hall, Inc.
Designed by R studio T
Cover design by Atif Toor
Photo research by Laura Miller

ISBN 0-439-42981-1

12 11 10 9 8 7 6 5 4 3 2 1   3 4 5 6 7 8/0

Printed in the U.S.A.
First printing, March 2003

Contents

Awesome Animals

Introduction

Awesome Ideas

Robert Ripley published his first Believe It or Not! cartoon at the New York *Globe*. It was such a success that by 1922, his readership had reached 80 million. Many people wrote to Ripley, hoping he would use their ideas in one of his cartoons.

In 1937, a boy named Charles Schulz sent Ripley a cartoon about the ability of his dog

A HUNTING DOG THAT EATS *PINS, TACKS, SCREWS AND RAZOR BLADES* IS OWNED BY C.F. SCHULZ, St. Paul, Minn.

Sparky to eat pins, tacks, screws, and razor blades. Schulz would go on to publish a whole comic strip starring Sparky, called *Peanuts*. Sparky's fictional name? Snoopy, of course.

Sparky is just one of hundreds of animals whose stories can be found in the Ripley archives. When you consider that Ripley spent much of his life seeking out the remarkable, the bizarre, the mysterious, and the unexplainable, it's no wonder that so many animals have found their way into his Believe It or Not! cartoons.

What could be more bizarre than a miniature Seeing Eye pony wearing sneakers? Or more mysterious than dolphins appearing out of the blue to save a stranger from drowning? Or more unexplainable than a dog that goes and sits by the door to wait for its owner—not when she pulls into the driveway, but as soon as she leaves the hospital where she works? And, of course, the dog that rescued 92 passengers from a grounded ship during a storm certainly qualifies as remarkable.

You'll find lots of stories like these in *Awesome Animals*. You'll also get a chance to test your own animal smarts by answering the Creature Feature quizzes and the Brain Busters in each chapter. And don't forget to take the Pop Quiz at the end of the book. Finally, put your scores together to find out your Ripley's Rank!

Now, get ready to enter the amazing world of animals. You might just discover that they are a lot smarter, braver, and more unbelievable than you thought!

Believe It!®

Not long ago, scientists thought that only humans could use tools. But recent studies have shown that some animals not only use tools, they also behave like humans in other ways.

Smashed Eggs: The Egyptian vulture eats disgusting stuff like garbage and lion dung, but it also likes ostrich eggs. The shells, however, are too tough to peck open, and the eggs are much too big for vultures to pick up and drop onto a rock from the air. This clever bird grabs a stone with its beak, lifts it up, and throws it down hard at the egg. And it keeps doing it again and again until the egg cracks.

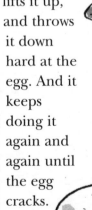

Creature Feature

When an elephant's trunk hangs down with the tip curled in, the elephant is probably saying it is . . .

a. happy.
b. bored.
c. frightened.
d. angry.

Cracking Up:

Chimpanzees love panda nuts. The trouble is, the nuts are almost impossible to crack open. Amazingly, some bands of African chimps have figured it out. The chimps carefully select heavy stones with naturally formed handles to use as hammers. Next, they set up nut-cracking stations, using tree roots or stumps to pound the nuts open on. Finally, they practice their technique over and over again— pound too lightly and the nut won't crack; pound too hard and the nut gets pulverized. It takes about seven years for a chimp to master the process, but once it does, it can open as many as 100 panda nuts a day.

Sew Cozy: Tailorbirds

punch holes around the edges of leaves with their beaks. Then they stitch the sides together with grass to make a cozy pocket— the perfect nest to raise their chicks in.

Creature Feature

While hunting for food among the sharp-edged coral reefs, porpoises often cover their tender noses with face masks they fashion out of . . .

a. sponges.
b. mud.
c. clamshells.
d. seaweed.

Toolin' Around:

Chimpanzees use tools to help them capture insect prey. They find twigs that are long and sturdy enough to poke into termite mounds. The termites scurry out, and the chimps scoop them into their mouths. There's nothing like a crunchy snack!

Shell Game: Abalone shells can be hard to break open. But that doesn't stop sea otters from getting inside them. While floating on its back, the otter sets a flat rock on its stomach. Then it bangs the abalone on the rock. The shell cracks open, and the otter dines on its favorite seafood.

Wireless: Workers at Blair Drummond Wildlife Park in Stirling, Scotland, got annoyed when they began getting prank calls—until they figured out who the culprit was. A chimpanzee named Chippy had swiped the chief game warden's

cell phone and, while his caregivers were sleeping, he pressed speed dial, waking them up in the middle of the night. It wasn't until he let out one of his signature screeches that his cover was blown. Now that his phone privileges have been suspended, Chippy is working on new ways to drive his caretakers bananas!

Tickled Pink: Rats are having fun at Ohio's Bowling Green State University psychology lab. With the help of ultrasonic devices, Jaak Panksepp discovered that rats make distinct chirping noises when they play with each other. When he tickled the rats on the back of the neck, the chirping noises increased. For Panksepp, who has been studying emotions for more than 20 years, this discovery was no laughing matter!

Counting on Isaac: Isaac is a golden retriever that can add, subtract, multiply, divide, and even do square roots. When Isaac was a pup, his owner, Gary Wimer, spent 20 minutes a day teaching him to count. The puppy loved his lessons and soon began astounding everyone who came into contact with him. All Wimer has to do is ask the little genius what the square root of 36 is, and Isaac will bark six times. He even helps Wimer's eight-year-old with his arithmetic. Imagine having a dog that can help you with your homework!

Creature Feature

Most rats will do anything to avoid becoming a cat snack. But once in a while, a rat will find itself irresistibly drawn to a cat because it . . .

a. wants to make friends.
b. wants to share the cat food.
c. is infected with *Toxoplasma gondii.*
d. is schizophrenic.

...I'll see you tomorrow!

Bird Brainiac: When Irene Pepperberg, a professor at the University of Arizona, says good night, she typically hears the reply, "Bye. I'm gonna go eat dinner. I'll see you tomorrow." Though the response is not unusual, the source is. It comes from Alex, an African gray parrot, Pepperberg's main research subject for more than 20 years. Alex has a 100-word vocabulary and can identify 50 different objects—not just by name, but also by how they are similar to one another. Pepperberg's study has proven that Alex is not merely "parroting" what he hears but is actually processing information.

A Beautiful Mind:
Koko, a lowland gorilla, has a vocabulary of more than 1,000 signs and understands 2,000 words of spoken English. A participant in the Gorilla Language Project, Koko has an IQ between 70 and 95. (One hundred is considered average for humans.) Koko is imaginative as well as smart. When playing with her dolls, she arranges their arms and hands in certain positions and pretends that they are signing, too!

Pulling Strings: Bernd Heinrich is a zoologist who specializes in studying ravens. One thing he's discovered is that they're very intelligent. Their results on the IQ tests he gives them are proof. Heinrich attaches a long string with a piece of food at the end to a high perch. To get to the food, a raven will have to repeat one step 30 times in a row. The bird has to lift up a length of string with one foot, then hold it down with the other foot while it pulls up a second length. It must repeat the process over and over again until it gets to the end of the string. Heinrich has found that most ravens can figure out how to do this within minutes.

Creature Feature

Sheep can tell which animals are other sheep . . .

a. when they are shown photos.
b. by the shape of their eyes.
c. through ESP (extrasensory perception).
d. even when blindfolded.

Screen Test:

Washington Zoo biologist Rob Shumaker is teaching words to orangutans. Azy, a 21-year-old male is his best student. Even Azy's mistakes show how smart he is. When presented with closed bags containing chopped fruit and asked to find the matching symbol on a computer screen, Azy picked a cup instead of a bag—a mistake that shows he is capable of organizing words into categories!

Little Squealer:

When a New York City restaurant owner was murdered on July 12, 1942, his green parrot told police the name of the killer. The bird had been taught to identify patrons by name, so when the parrot kept repeating the same name over and over, the police knew they had their man!

Creature Feature

Ospreys, which are also called fish hawks, locate good places to fish by . . .

a. catching the scent of fish on the thermals that rise up from the sea.
b. watching the flight patterns of other birds.
c. following fishing boats.
d. listening for splashes as they fly over the water.

Something to Crow About:

What does a crow do when it has too much to carry? One clever crow in Washington's Olympic Mountains was observed with this problem. On the ground were several crackers that the crow wanted all for itself. Each time it picked one up and then opened its beak to get another, the first cracker fell out of its mouth. That's when the crow did some pretty awesome problem-solving. It propped the crackers very close together—like sliced bread—in the snow. Then it opened wide and grabbed all seven in its beak at once!

Name That Tune:

Trainers at a German zoo taught a female elephant to identify several tunes. Though they tried to stump her by varying speeds, changing rhythms, and using different instruments, the elephant still recognized every one. In another experiment, she was taught to match patterns on cards. Six hundred pairs of cards later, she got a perfect score—even after a year had passed!

Mathpanzee: Dr. Sally Boysen, director of the Primate Cognition Center of Ohio State University, is teaching chimpanzees about numbers. One day, she dropped three peaches in one box and three in another. Then she took out number cards and asked Sheba, one of the chimps, how many peaches were in the boxes. When Sheba pointed to six, Boysen was astounded. Though the chimp had been taught to recognize numbers and to put them in order, she had never been taught to count or add!

Piggin' Out: Professor Stanley Curtis at Pennsylvania State University has proved that pigs are extremely observant creatures with excellent memories. How? By teaching them to play video games. Using their snouts to control the joysticks, six pigs—Ebony, Ivory, Pork, Beans, Jekyll, and Hyde—started out by moving the cursor through simple mazes. Then they went on to more complex games where they had to match similar objects or hit a target that got smaller and smaller. Of course, the pigs were well motivated: Their efforts were instantly rewarded with M&Ms.

Putting Their Feet Down: Zoologists from Stanford University have discovered that elephants have a unique way of communicating over long distances. How do they do it? With a series of stomps that send vibrations rippling through the ground. The vibrations are picked up at the other end by the receiving elephants' toenails, then travel up their bones to the elephants' ears. Typical messages are warnings that danger is near and have been heeded by elephants as far as 20 miles away!

Creature Feature

Though no one noticed when King Henry III's pet parrot, whose wings were clipped, fell into the Thames River, it was saved because it . . .

a. squawked "boat."
b. knew how to doggy paddle.
c. squawked "help!"
d. wore a mini life preserver.

Cat Burglar: When citizens in Guelph, Ontario, Canada, started to notice that some of their things were missing, they suspected that a burglar was afoot. But what kind of bandit would steal gloves, shirts, shoes, toys, and even a

bag of potatoes? Amber Queen cracked the case when she found Moo, her 15-pound cat, trying to drag some of the missing items through her cat door. Moo hasn't reformed, but Queen makes every effort to return the loot by placing ads in the local newspaper and putting up lists of stolen items around town. Luckily for Moo, no one has tried to press charges—yet!

Scrambled Eggs: For years, scientists have known that the cuckoo lays its eggs in other birds' nests to avoid the wing-breaking work of raising its chicks. But they haven't been sure why the magpies are such willing foster mothers. Now they know that a cuckoo will fly by to check the nest and make sure that the magpie hasn't tossed the cuckoo egg out. If it has, the cuckoo will destroy the nest and all the magpie's eggs or chicks!

Cat Attack: Lions specialize in cooperative hunting. But who knew that they were smart enough to plan their strategy ahead of time? Dr. Donald Griffin, who studies animals in the wild, watched four female lions go after a wildebeest. To distract the herd, two of the lions deliberately placed themselves where the wildebeests could see them. The third lion crawled through the grass until she was midway between the lions and herd and crouched, unseen. The fourth lion charged from behind the herd, sending the animals running toward the hidden lion, who burst from cover and killed one of the wildebeests. All four lions shared in the kill!

Creature Feature

Darrel is a chimpanzee who can . . .

a. write his name.
b. play checkers.
c. win video games.
d. understand fractions.

Pop Singers:

Scientists eavesdropping on black-capped chickadees have discovered that the males of the species regularly have singing contests! Female chickadees are the judges. The male with the loudest, most aggressive-sounding song is the winner. His prize? He gets to mate with the most females. Scientists have proved this theory by genetically testing chicks for paternity. As expected, the best singers had fathered the most chicks!

By the Book: Danny Younger, a parakeet owned by Ella Hohenstein of St. Louis, Missouri, flew the coop. Four weeks later, the bird was returned home. Because the bird kept repeating his name, the people who found him decided to see if his last name was in the telephone book. Sure enough, they found an identical listing—which was for Hohenstein's grandson after whom the parakeet was named.

Creature Feature

Sparkie Williams, a parrot, knows 531 words and can . . .

a. perform a high-wire act.
b. play the flute.
c. recite eight nursery rhymes.
d. build castles with Lego toys.

Think Tanks: Scientists have always believed that invertebrates (animals without backbones) are at the bottom of the IQ scale, capable of little more than the most basic survival skills. Yet the octopuses at the Seattle Aquarium appeared to be playing—a behavior that requires a considerable amount of thinking! So marine biologists Roland Anderson and Jennifer Mather decided to place empty bottles in the octopuses' tanks and watch to see what they would do. "One blew the bottle back and forth against a water inlet, a little like bouncing a ball, and one blew the bottle around the tank," said Anderson. It looks like some invertebrates are smarter than people thought—except for the folks at the Ripley's Aquarium in South Carolina. One octopus there figured out how to open its tank, crawl out, and eat the fish in the next tank, then return to its own tank and close it, fooling everyone until it was finally caught in the act!

Mud-Packers: Work elephants in Myanmar have been known to stuff the bells around their necks with mud. Why? So that the bells won't ring when the elephants sneak out at night to steal the bananas they love to eat!

Creature Feature

Ken Allen, who lives at the San Diego Zoo, is . . .

a. an orangutan that regularly dismantles its cage.
b. a koala that picks the lock on its cage.
c. a gorilla that can turn off its electrified fence.
d. a lemur that can slip through the bars of its cage.

I t can be a real *beast* trying to tell the difference between fact and fiction—especially when the truth is so bizarre. Think you're up to the challenge?

Robert Ripley dedicated his life to seeking out the bizarre and unusual. But every unbelievable thing he recorded was known to be true. In the Brain Busters at the end of every chapter, you'll play Ripley's role—trying to verify the fantastic facts presented. Each Ripley's Brain Buster contains a group of four shocking statements. But of these so-called "facts," **one** is **fiction**. Will you **Believe It!** or **Not!**?

Wait—there's more! Following the Brain Busters are special bonus questions in which you'll try to solve one more "wildlife wonder." to see how you rate, flip to the end of the book for answer keys and a scorecard.

Human nature? **Lots of animals have abilities similar to humans'. Three of the following examples are true and one is false. Can you spot the one bogus animal behavior?**

a. When a beekeeper dies, his or her bees will often use their amazing navigational skills to find their keeper's grave and say "good-bye" to their old master.
              Believe It!   **Not!**

b. All porcupines can float.

Believe It!　　　　**Not!**

c. Despite its size, a black rhinoceros can outrun most human sprinters.

Believe It!　　　　**Not!**

d. Piranhas will actually gather together for meals around rocks that they use like tables.

Believe It!　　　　**Not!**

• •

BONUS QUESTION—WILDLIFE WONDER

A baby gray whale drinks a lot of milk! How much? Enough to fill more than 2,000 bottles a day.

Believe It!　　　　**Not!**

Some jobs are so highly specialized that only a nonhuman can do them.

Photo Finish: In Fort Collins, Colorado, David Costlow, owner of a white-water rafting company, has solved one very vexing problem. Part of his service is providing customers with a photograph to remember their trip by. The trouble is,

because of the steep, winding canyon roads, it often takes longer to get the film developed than it does to complete the entire white-water adventure! So Costlow straps tiny backpacks to pigeons, who fly the film over the canyon to base camp so the pictures can be developed by the time the rafters return!

Creature Feature

Old Pete, who guards a flock of sheep at a prison farm in South America, is a . . .

a. 300-pound ostrich.
b. three-legged Old English sheepdog.
c. 500-pound gorilla.
d. seven-ton elephant.

23

Spitting Image: After Michael Riding lost 20 sheep to coyotes in just one year, he decided to get them a bodyguard—one that was fierce, loyal, and protective. Enter Ping, a llama with all those

qualities and more. Coyotes hunt by separating one sheep from the rest. When Ping senses danger, he circles the flock to keep all of the sheep together. If one sheep begins to stray, Ping will spit and hiss to make it behave. In the five years that Ping's been on the job, Riding has lost no more than two sheep a year.

Scratch and Sniff: Extremely active dogs don't necessarily make the best pets, but they do make terrific drug-detectors. Trained to patrol heavily trafficked areas such as airports, bus depots, and sports arenas, one dog can inspect up to 500 packages, suitcases, and backpacks in less than 30 minutes—a job that would take a person several days. In mailrooms and airports, dogs even have to jump on moving conveyor belts. During his career, Chopper, a 10-year veteran of the Customs Service, found more than 80 million dollars worth of smuggled drugs! Retired now, he lives a quiet life with his handler.

DRESSED FOR SUCCESS

Court Jousters: Jeff de Boer of Canada makes authentic medieval armor for cats and mice.

Bit Parts:
Eddie Diijon's Flea Circus opened with a chariot race, followed by the high-wire act. For the finale, a cannon shot the tiny daredevils through a ring of fire. But not to worry, they always landed safely.

The Canadian National Exhibition PRESENTS EDDIE DIIJON'S

FLEA CIRCUS

SEE THE FIRST FLEA CIRCUS IN CANADA FOR 47 YEARS

FEATURING
Paddy
The Tap Dancing Flea

Coat Tales:
In case you can't tell what it is, this feline owned by Larry Heaney of Maryland comes complete with a label: The word *cat* spelled out in its fur.

Creative

Clawing Her Way to Fame: Tillamook Cheddar uses her claws and teeth to create paintings. By the age of three, this well-known canine artist had already done six solo art shows in New York and California.

Paper Trail: In 1910, the Paris art critics gave high praise to Boronali's Sunset on the Adriatic Sea. Only later did they learn that Boronali was a donkey who painted with a brush tied to his tail.

Watercolors: Sunset Sam, a dolphin who lived at the Clearwater Marine Aquarium in Florida, held a paintbrush in his mouth to create pictures.

Critters

Trunk Show: To raise money for the Thai Elephant Conservation Center in Lampang, conductors Richard Lair and Dave Soldier taught 12 elephants to play in an orchestra!

Acting Up: He may not be a household name, but Aurthur, a 15-year-old lion, is a lifelong movie and TV star. You've probably seen him in such films as *Ace Ventura* and *Born Free,* and as the MGM lion. Aurthur also helps raise money for T.I.G.E.R.S., a wildlife preservation group in South Carolina, where he lives.

ZOOLOGY
Hall of Fame

Tall and Tan: Reaching a height of 19 feet, the giraffe is the tallest animal on Earth. A giraffe baby can grow an astonishing half-inch per hour!

Big Daddy: Male mountain gorillas are the largest of all primates. A mature silverback may weigh up to 600 pounds, have an arm span of eight feet, and the strength of eight strong men!

Bigger Mama: The blue whale is the largest mammal ever known. The heaviest on record is a female that tipped the scale at more than 200 tons. The longest recorded length is more than 100 feet.

Fast-Forward: Clocking in at 65 miles per hour, the cheetah is the fastest known animal. This amazing runner can accelerate from zero to 60 miles per hour in just three seconds—faster than many cars!

Slow Motion: The slowest mammal is the three-toed sloth. On the ground, it can only travel up to eight feet per minute. At that rate, it would take 27.5 hours to travel one mile. Up in the trees, however, the sloth may reach a speedy 15 feet per minute!

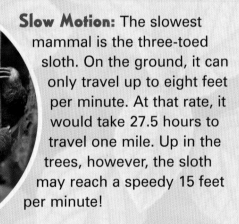

Mini Me: The pygmy mouse lemur weighs in at a whopping one-tenth of an ounce—less than some beetles weigh.

Heroic Tales

Saved by a Bullet: In 2000, the Sica family paid $5,000 for an operation to save the life of Bullet, their 13-year-old golden retriever. Two years later, Bullet repaid

the favor by alerting the Sicas when their three-week-old son began to choke. Had the paramedics arrived just ten seconds later, the baby would have died.

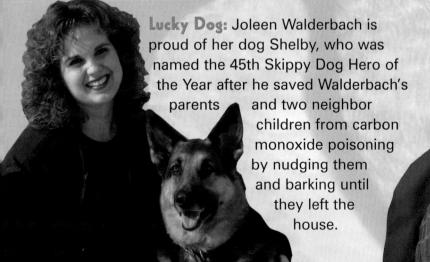

Lucky Dog: Joleen Walderbach is proud of her dog Shelby, who was named the 45th Skippy Dog Hero of the Year after he saved Walderbach's parents and two neighbor children from carbon monoxide poisoning by nudging them and barking until they left the house.

Hairy Situation: When a small boy fell into the gorilla pit at an Illinois zoo, Binti Jua, an eight-year-old female gorilla, gently carried him to the workers' door, where humans took over the rescue.

Tail Break: A baby kangaroo rescued by Nigel Etherington of Perth, Australia, later saved Etherington from a fire by banging its tail on a door until he awoke and escaped.

Wake-up Call: Lynn Norely didn't have an electronic smoke detector to wake her up when her house caught fire, but she did have a parrot named Rupert, whose loud squawking did the job. Now she lectures on the importance of smoke alarms and brings "Super Rupert" along to do his impression of what they sound like.

Paw Power

Wired! The U.S. Space Command in Colorado used a ferret named Misty to help rewire a new computerized command center.

The Nose Knows: Statistics show that a certified working dog can sniff out the tiniest amount of explosives more than 90 percent of the time. Until technology comes up with a machine more sensitive than a canine nose, trained dogs will be a regular sight at airports and other public places.

TRES PASSERS
WILL BE
EATEN
SEC. 13   CHAP. 34
CODE 1954

Earning His Stripes: It's a safe bet that there weren't many trespassers when this tiger was on duty as a security guard at the Des Moines Zoo in Iowa.

Making Scents: A trained bomb-sniffing dog can find very small amounts of explosives within minutes. Unlike drug-sniffing dogs, they have to stay very calm so they won't accidentally set off any explosives. In 1972, a Los Angeles-bound Boeing 707 turned around and returned to John F. Kennedy Airport after someone called in a bomb threat. Brandy, a German shepherd who worked with the local police department, was on the job. In short order, she located a bomb made of C-4, a powerful plastic explosive, inside a briefcase—just 12 minutes before it was set to go off.

Creature Feature

Teddy, a calico cat owned by Kathleen Calligan of Huntsville, Alabama, is . . .

a. an ordained minister.
b. the town mayor.
c. a school mascot.
d. a dogcatcher.

Techno Rat: Dr. Judy Reevis, an information technologist, wanted to hook up an old classroom to the Internet. The cramped space above the ceiling made it impossible for her to do the wiring herself, so she decided to train a rat to do the work. First, she tied a string around a rat named Ratty and attached the other end to a line  of cable. She then sent Ratty, who can pull up to 250 feet of cable at a time, through the ceiling to do his job. Dr. Reevis knocked on the ceiling to keep him moving in the right direction. To date, Ratty has wired ten schools.

Who's the Boss? Before it can be on the job full-time, a Seeing Eye dog has to learn how to take various paths around obstacles, judge heights so it can prevent its human from bumping into low overhead objects like branches and awnings, and understand commands such as left, right, stop, and forward. But, by far, the most important lesson a guide dog must learn is to disobey! Many dogs have saved their owners' life by refusing a command that would place them in the path of danger.

Top Dog: Allen Parton suffers from memory loss and partial paralysis sustained during the Gulf War. With the help of Canine Partners for Independence in Hampshire, England, Parton and Endal, his Labrador retriever, have developed a special sign

language. When Parton forgets the names of things, all he has to do is tap his head, touch his cheek, or rub his hands together, and Endal will fetch his hat, his razor, or his gloves, respectively. The dog can also help shop, withdraw money from an ATM (automated teller machine), and load and unload the washer and dryer!

Creature Feature

In the 1960s, mail was carried over the Dead Heart desert in Australia by . . .

a. a kangaroo with a pouch full of letters.
b. six dingoes pulling a cart.
c. camels pulling a car with no engine.
d. a pack of koalas.

Slow but Sure: Juan Solis of Bolivia was totally blind. Luckily, he had a smart four-legged friend to help him out—a giant tortoise who led Solis safely around town.

No Horsing Around:

Cuddles, a miniature horse just two feet tall, is the first guide horse for the blind in the United States. Cuddles's training by the Guide Horse Foundation was put to the test when she and her owner, Dan Shaw, passed through New York City on the way to her new home in Maine. Clad in tiny sneakers to keep her from slipping, Cuddles took the busy streets and noisy subways right in stride.

Dog-eared: What happens when an emergency vehicle comes screeching down the road behind a driver who is deaf? In the absence of a hearing human passenger, a specially trained dog seated next to a deaf driver is the perfect solution. The dog alerts its human by gently placing a paw on his or her leg. At home, the dog will nuzzle its owner awake and alert him or her to other sound signals, such as a doorbell, a crying baby, or a smoke alarm.

Speedy Delivery:

Sending messages by pigeon dates back to ancient times. During World War II, radio and telegraph messages could be intercepted, so the United States used 56,000 of these swift birds, which can fly 70 miles per hour and cover 700 miles a day, to carry important communications from place to place.

Cap and Bone: Darcy James, a four-year-old German shepherd guide dog, graduated from Mississippi State University with her mistress, Barbara James. In recognition of the splendid job Darcy did leading Barbara from class to class, university officials awarded her special academic honors. Darcy, however, was much more interested in the doggy treats she also received as her reward.

Creature Feature

A building erected by monks in Compiègne, France, is called the Abbey of . . .

a. Bear Field, because a trained bear was used to clear the construction site.
b. Canine Comfort, because the monks trained dogs to provide aid to the residents of a leper colony.
c. Feline Friendship, because the monks had 150 cats to keep the abbey from being overrun by mice.
d. Canine Guidance, because the monks were blind and depended on Seeing Eye dogs to guide them.

Bright Idea: For some people who are paralyzed, capuchin monkeys serve as all-around lifelines. Trained by an organization called Helping Hands, a capuchin monkey will fetch an object that its owner points to with a laser light. The light, which is attached to a wheelchair, can be manipulated by a person's mouth. The monkey can turn pages of a book, open a refrigerator, pop the top of a prepared beverage and insert a straw, unwrap a sandwich, feed its owner, and even scratch an annoying itch!

Creature Feature

In 1917, as part of the World War I conservation effort, sheep were used to . . .

a. pull schoolchildren in carts to conserve fuel.
b. trim the White House lawn.
c. provide families with milk.
d. guard army camps at night.

Clean Sweep: An elephant owned by the Duke of Devonshire, England, was trained to wet down the walks of a park with a watering can and then sweep them with a broom.

Canine Delivery:

For a three-year period in the late 1800s, a German shepherd dog named Dorsey was the only mail carrier between the towns of Calico and Bismarck in California's Mojave Desert. Dorsey never once missed his regular schedule on the three-mile trip.

Deep Snout: Luise,
a 250-pound wild boar, has been trained by German police to root out hidden drugs that even dogs can't find. Her sense of smell is so acute that she can locate drugs buried under four feet of earth.

Monkey Business: Dore Schary was the production head of the MGM Studios from 1948 to 1956. But when he first started out as a young writer at Columbia Pictures, Schary worked on a jungle movie in which a monkey was paid more for one day of work than Schary received for a week.

Creature Feature

At the court of King Louis XVI, the entertainment often included . . .

a. trained poodles jumping through hoops of fire.

b. costumed parrots singing opera.

c. monkeys in tuxedos playing flutes.

d. pigs in pantaloons dancing to bagpipes.

Crazy creatures! **Some animals have abilities that humans only dream of. Can you spot the one amazing animal fact that's incredibly untrue?**

a. When the risk of attack is high, mallard ducks will sleep with one eye open and half of their brain "awake." They sleep normally when the risk is low.

Believe It!   **Not!**

b. A grizzly bear's nose knows! These big tough guys have such a powerful sense of smell that they can detect a human who is two miles away!

Believe It!   **Not!**

c. Not only can an owl see in the dark, it can also see behind itself by using the extra set of eyes in the back of its head.

Believe It!   **Not!**

d. An aardvark can dig its way through a termite mound (a feat in itself!). But even more impressive is its thick skin—which allows it to feel no pain, even when the termites start stinging!

Believe It!   **Not!**

BONUS QUESTION—WILDLIFE WONDER

Many lizards have a third eye in the back of their head, though in some species it is more developed than in others.

Believe It!   **Not!**

The connections formed between animals of different species can sometimes seem downright magical.

Milk Maid: When a stray cat broke its leg in a fight, Susan Trumblay took her to an animal hospital to recuperate, and took the cat's three-week-old kittens home. Trumblay thought she was going to have to feed the little ones formula with an eyedropper. But her female Pomeranian dog, who had never even had a litter of puppies, had other ideas. Amazingly, the little dog began to produce milk and nursed the kittens herself!

Creature Feature

A cat owned by A. W. Mitchell of Vancouver, British Columbia, nurtured . . .

a. six baby Canada geese.
b. 25 chicks.
c. three baby raccoons.
d. eight newborn rats.

Mistaken Identity:

Lisa Embree was in her backyard when she found an abandoned baby squirrel. Embree tried to feed the baby with a dropper, but the squirrel would have none of it. That's when Embree had a brilliant idea. Her cat, Princess, had five babies of her own. Why not give her a sixth? Lisa's experiment was a "purrfect" success. Katherine Houpt, a Cornell University animal expert, said that it is not unusual for a cat to accept a foster child, but that Embree should not be surprised if the squirrel grows up believing it's a cat!

Mr. Mom:
Six chicks were adopted by a rooster owned by Mary E. Harris of Tacoma, Washington. When the mother hen disappeared, the rooster rounded up the chicks, fed them, and then warmed and protected them.

Creature Feature

Yanto, a six-year-old who lives in Jakarta, Indonesia, frequently sleeps with the family pet, which is a . . .

a. panther.
b. monkey.
c. baby elephant.
d. python.

Body Heat: Cara Fligstein was buying pet food when she spied a cat and six nursing kittens nestled in a box in a corner of the pet store. A seventh kitten, much smaller than the rest, was too weak to nurse. Never

one to resist a kitten in need, Fligstein bought kitten formula and whisked the starving baby to the vet. The diagnosis? Severe dehydration. The kitten would have to be fed hourly and kept warm. Fligstein was assembling blankets and a heating pad when she realized that she wouldn't need them after all. Linus, her cairn terrier, was already keeping the kitten warm by allowing her to sleep on him. Three years later, Linus and Angel, the cat, are still the best of friends.

Mixed Company: Cattle and sheep usually don't mix, but when a group of lambs was penned in the same

pasture with cattle, the two species bonded so much that the cattle actually protected the sheep from predators.

The Fox and the Hound:

Foxhounds are trained to hunt foxes. But the foxhound and fox at the Belstone Hunt in England are an exception. Best buddies, the two animals follow each other around, eating and sleeping together and even drinking water from the same dish.

Blind Faith: A victim of animal abuse, Little Ben, a Jack Russell terrier, is totally blind. People at the shelter in Essex, England, that rescued him were afraid he'd have to be put to sleep. But that was before Bill, another Jack Russell terrier, decided to befriend Ben. Bill allowed Ben to hang onto the back of his neck while he led him around the kennel to water and food dishes. When the local news stations broadcast the story, the shelter received more than 5,000 phone calls from people wanting to adopt the pair of dogs. It wasn't long before they were taken in by a woman with a big backyard and another little dog named Rosie to keep them company.

Horse Sense: Clever Hans, a horse, lived during the early 1900s. His owner, a math professor named Wilhelm von Osten, taught Hans how to spell and do simple mathematical problems. When von Osten tested his horse's knowledge, Clever Hans would nod his head for "yes," shake his head for "no," and stomp his feet to count out numbers. Visitors were amazed at how often Hans answered questions correctly. But then someone noticed that Hans only answered correctly if the questioner already knew the answer. It seems that Hans did not really know the answers, but was so sensitive to his human audience that he was able to pick up clues from a raised eyebrow, a sigh, or even a tilt of the head. Most people would consider that behavior quite clever as well!

Creature Feature

Dr. Hywell Williams of King's College Hospital in London has a patient who was alerted by her dog that she had . . .

a. severe bad breath.
b. athlete's foot.
c. tooth decay.
d. skin cancer.

Seizing the Moment: Because people with epilepsy often lose control of their bodies during a seizure, it's important for them to be somewhere safe. Epileptics have no idea when a seizure will strike, but research shows that dogs of various breeds, sizes, and ages are able to predict seizures. How they do it remains a mystery, but dogs like Brian Revheim's English setter, Arthur, can be trained to alert their owners minutes before an attack occurs.

Scents-sational! Dog-trainer Duane Pickel has trained a schnauzer named George to sniff out cancer before it can become a threat. After 8,000 hours of training, this talented canine correctly detected melanoma, the most dangerous form of skin cancer, 400 times out of 401 attempts.

Creature Feature

Penny, a Doberman pinscher, alerts her owner that she is about to have a seizure by . . .

a. pushing her into a chair.
b. bringing her a pillow.
c. banging on the piano.
d. hiding her car keys.

Sixth Scents: In his book, *Dogs That Know When Their Owners Are Coming Home,* Rupert Sheldrake writes about telepathic behavior between animals and their owners. One of his subjects, an English hospital worker named Gloria Batabyal, was  puzzled by the fact that her husband always had a piping hot cup of tea waiting for her when she arrived home, even though her schedule was unpredictable. How did he know when to put the kettle on? The couple's two dogs always ran to the window at the exact moment she left the hospital, giving her husband just enough time to prepare the tea.

Phoning Home: When Veronica Rowe's daughter Marian left for college, she had no choice but to leave

her adoring cat, Carlo, home with her family. Mysteriously, whenever she called, Carlo would perk up and rush over to the phone before anyone had even answered. No one else ever knew when Marian was phoning, but Carlo's instincts were right every time!

Sweet Homecoming:

Sugar, a cream-colored Persian cat, is the star of a study published by J. B. Rhine of Duke University. Of all the cases he documented in which animals find their owners over long distances, Rhine was most impressed by Sugar, who jumped out of the family car and disappeared before they moved from California to Oklahoma. One day, Sugar just showed up at her owners' new home, having traveled 1,000 miles to find them!

Visiting Hours: During the 1960s, a 12-year boy from West Virginia found a racing pigeon in his backyard. It was wearing a leg ring with the number 167. After the boy fed it, the pigeon stuck around and soon became the boy's pet. No one knew how devoted the bird had become until the boy was hospitalized 105 miles from home. Recovering from an operation in his room, the boy heard a familiar noise at the window. He asked the nurse to open the window, and in flew a pigeon. On its leg was a ring with the number 167!

Prince of Tides: During World War I, when Private James Brown of England was sent overseas to France, his dog, Prince, was heartbroken. Imagine Brown's surprise when Prince came trotting up to him in the trenches! No one could figure out how the dog got there. The only possible explanation was that Prince had boarded a ship full of soldiers wearing the same uniform as his master. Brown's commanding officer was so impressed by the dog's loyalty that he allowed Prince to stay by his master's side for the rest of the war!

Creature Feature

At the Anderson House Hotel in Wabash, Minnesota, visitors can . . .

a. bring their pets into the restaurant.
b. request pet-sitting service.
c. milk the cows for fresh milk in the morning.
d. reserve a cat to keep them company for the night.

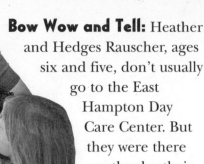

Bow Wow and Tell: Heather and Hedges Rauscher, ages six and five, don't usually go to the East Hampton Day Care Center. But they were there on the day their mother had a meeting, and volunteers from the Animal Rescue Fund brought dogs in to show the children. When the dogs arrived, Heather cried, "That's Cody!" It turned out that Cody had disappeared from the girls' home three months earlier. The folks at the animal shelter said that Cody hadn't acted like a stray, wagging his tail or licking visitors. Maybe he was just waiting for a day like this one!

Horseback Therapy: Patients at the Akron Children's Hospital in Ohio look forward to the days when a miniature horse named Petie comes to visit. Petie gives them rides or pulls them down the hall in their wheelchairs, his handlers walking alongside.

Creature Feature

It has been demonstrated that stroking a pet can . . .

a. lower blood pressure.
b. cure mental illness.
c. induce weight loss.
d. increase one's IQ.

Fin-tastic! Dolphins have enchanted people for thousands of years. Now there is evidence that young people who suffer from autism and have serious trouble bonding with others show marked improvement when in the company of these playful creatures. Dolphins seem to be able to sense just what autistic children need and are less rambunctious with them than they are with their trainers. After just a few sessions, Rafi, an 18-year-old autistic patient at the Aytanim home for the handicapped in Israel, spoke a few words for the first time in his life.

Puppy Love: Gayle Bardin-Aversa, an occupational therapist with Therapy Dogs International, says that she can get better results from patients when she uses a six-year-old Yorkshire terrier named Zoey. For example, one four-year-old boy found it painful to use his disabled left hand and no one could get him to try. But when Bardin-Aversa placed Zoey in the boy's lap and asked him to brush her, he eagerly grasped the brush with his left hand. Clearly, Zoey had provided more motivation than anyone else could.

Horsing Around:

Taking pet devotion to new heights, The Maltese Cat, a thoroughbred race horse, was chosen by his trainer, Terry Lee Griffith of Stanton, Delaware, to be the best man at his wedding. The horse wore formal attire, including a top hat!

Creature Feature

Bred in Australia, a new type of dog combining the friendliness of one breed with the intelligence of a poodle is called a . . .

a. schnoodle (schnauzer and poodle).
b. labradoodle (Labrador retriever and poodle).
c. cockapoo (cocker spaniel and poodle).
d. pugadoodle (pug and poodle).

Chimp Change:

When an elderly Danish woman died, she left her entire life savings to six creatures who were dear to her heart. Jimmy, Trunto, Trine, Fifi, Grimmi, and Gigi, chimpanzees at the Copenhagen Zoo, were suddenly $60,000 richer! Now that's a lot of bananas!

Big Woof: Now there's a must-have device for dog lovers who are experiencing a communication gap. The Bowlingual, available in Japan, claims to translate those meaningful woofs uttered by your pooch into human words! Tone, pitch, volume, and other barking  patterns are matched to canine emotions, which then appear as words on the Bowlingual computer screen.

Pampered Pet Set: The ad in the telephone book boasts air-conditioned private rooms for pampered pets as well as a fully furnished two-bedroom apartment. The Malibu Pet Hotel has something for everyone—everyone with four legs, that is. Furry guests enjoy daily five-mile walks, grooming, and lots of chew toys. Their wagging tails are certain to reassure two-legged owners that their pets are more than well cared for.

Pet Detective:

When Carol Piccione lost Shadow, her two-year-old black Labrador retriever mix, she was inconsolable. She went to the local animal shelter twice a day and circled the neighborhood in her car for days on end. She had

almost given up when, a month later, she was driving by another animal shelter farther from her home and something told her to go in. There was Shadow— Piccione had found him just 15 minutes before he was scheduled to be put to sleep! Not wanting others to go through what she did, Piccione started Animal Lost & Found, Inc. For a fee, Piccione will devote her considerable skills to locating a lost pet. Though she refuses to divulge her secrets, she pretty much has the process down to a science. Just ask the owners of Stella, Bowser, Cupcake, and Mischka!

Creature Feature

Pet detective Lori Ketcham's most unusual case involved locating a lost . . .

a. giraffe.
b. potbelly pig.
c. emu.
d. ferret.

Brain Buster

They say that opposites attract—and it seems especially true in the animal kingdom. But one of the following animal pairs stands alone—as being totally false!

a. Who would have thought that porcupines and coyotes could be the best of friends? Coyotes share their food with porcupines and, in exchange, their prickly buddies will happily scratch their backs.

Believe It!   Not!

b. Honeyguide birds need the help of honey badgers to retrieve sweet nectar from beehives. The bird will flutter around the badger until it digs out the honey from the hive, leaving the honeycomb for its feathered friend.

Believe It!   Not!

c. In 2002, people in Kenya were shocked to see a lioness mothering two baby oryxes, an animal she would normally eat for lunch.

Believe It!   Not!

d. In the shallow water of tide pools lives a strange pair—the blind shrimp and the goby. The shrimp digs the burrow that the two will share, while the goby keeps an eye out—because the shrimp can't see at all.

Believe It!   Not!

BONUS QUESTION—WILDLIFE WONDER

A penguin was brought from Greenland to the National Zoo in Washington, D.C. Lonesome for home, the penguin befriended a polar bear in the next cage over and refused to leave its side.

Believe It!   **Not!**

Many animal species are in danger of becoming extinct. It's a good thing that there are people devoted to keeping them alive.

Breeding Grounds: In recent years, the purpose of zoos has shifted from family entertainment to preserving species in danger of extinction—and with good reason. The tropical rain forest that contains the greatest percentage of the world's animal species is disappearing at a rate of 50 acres per minute!

Creature Feature

There are more of these animals in zoos today than in all of Asia.

a. Pandas
b. Siberian tigers
c. Rhesus monkeys
d. Red-crowned cranes

Frozen Zoo: The San Diego Zoo keeps some of their animals in freezers—not whole animals, of course, but their cells. Four storage tanks hold the cells of more than 4,000 animals. The cells are frozen in liquid

nitrogen to prevent the formation of ice crystals, which would tear the cells during thawing. Thawed without ice crystals, cells remain unharmed and can even grow again.

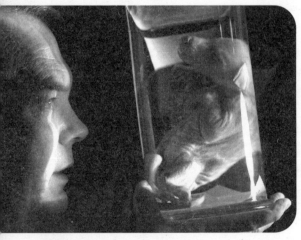

Coming Back to Life: In 1936, the Tasmanian tiger became extinct. Every last one had been hunted down by farmers who blamed the wolf-sized marsupial for killing their sheep. Recently, Mike Archer, director of the Australian Museum in Sydney, took steps to clone the animal. In May 2000, a research team extracted DNA from a pup that had been preserved in formaldehyde for the museum's collection. It may not be long until the call of the Tasmanian tiger is heard again.

Are You My Mommy? In 1986, there were only three California condors living in the wild and 12 others living at the Los Angeles Zoo. Hoping to increase their numbers, zoologists decided to try breeding them in captivity. In the wild, condors lay a single egg every other year. But at the zoo, their caregivers whisk the eggs away and put them into incubators, hoping that the condors will lay more. Because baby birds think that whoever feeds them is their parent, caregivers wear condor hand puppets so that the babies won't get attached to them. Today, there are 36 condors living in the wild and 115 in captivity.

Creature Feature

Without zoos and their breeding centers, this animal would be as dead as a dinosaur.

a. European bison
b. Bald eagle
c. Mountain gorilla
d. Hippopotamus

Bearing Up: A polar bear named Gus is the main attraction at the Central Park Zoo in New York City. But fame was not enough to make him happy. Obsessively swimming from one end of his pool to the other, Gus was clearly suffering from boredom. The zookeepers decided to cheer him up with a brand-new $25,000 Jacuzzi. Fighting the strong current and rushing water seemed to perk Gus up. But it was the "bearcicles," fish coated with peanut butter and frozen inside a block of ice, that really did wonders for his mood!

Scaredy Cat: In an effort to entertain Nikki, a Siberian tiger at the Oregon Zoo, caretakers put a trout in her pool. But although many tigers like to fish, Nikki ignored the fish—until it leaped out of the water. Startled, the big cat jumped right out of the pool! The ball her keepers gave her next was much more to her liking.

Creature Feature

Counting just mammals and birds, our planet loses one species every . . .

a. five years.
b. ten years.
c. 18 months.
d. eight months.

Well-Oiled Operation:

When a tanker spill polluted South African waters with oil in June 2000, the lives of more than 40,000 penguins were threatened. The oil that covered the penguins from head to toe stripped the feathers of their natural waterproofing, and left the penguins waterlogged and in danger of freezing. Thousands of volunteers worked as fast as they could to move the birds to the mainland, where they could be warmed up and fed. When the penguins were strong enough, volunteers scrubbed their feathers with soap and toothbrushes. As soon as water began to bead up on their feathers, the penguins were released. The biggest bird rescue ever attempted was a roaring success!

Hog Heaven: Diablo, a warthog at the San Antonio Zoo in Texas, got his name (which means "devil" in Spanish) from his habit of growling and charging at his caregivers. But everything changed when turnips and sweet potatoes were buried in his outdoor pen. Diablo kicked up his heels with joy as he gathered the hidden treats. Apparently he wasn't mean at all—just bored or hungry for his favorite foods.

Tons of Love:

Husband-and-wife team Scott Riddle and Heidi Strommer Riddle, former zookeepers from Los Angeles, have achieved their dream—Riddle's Elephant Breeding Farm and Wildlife Sanctuary in Arkansas. This nonprofit sanctuary takes in any elephant that needs a home, from retired circus performers to cantankerous zoo misfits. And then there's Solomon, an orphaned, unruly calf from Zimbabwe. Under the Riddles' care, he has morphed into a gentle giant who entertains visitors by playing the harmonica!

Marine Biology: The Kemp's Ridley turtle is the smallest and rarest of sea turtles. In fact, it's so scarce that the Mexican government sent Marines to guard the only beach on which it nests.

Creature Feature

In 1976, there were only about 5,000 harbor seals left in the wild. With the passage of the Marine Mammal Protection Act of 1972, which made it a crime to kill the seals, their numbers have increased to about . . .

a. 10,000.
b. 15,000.
c. 25,000.
d. 30,000.

Lofty Goal: When large fish hawks called ospreys wound up on the New York State endangered species list, some bird lovers went into the nest-building business. Ospreys had begun to disappear for two reasons. First, the use of the insecticide DDT weakened their eggs,

causing them to crack open before the chicks were ready to hatch. And second, because of a shortage of suitable nesting areas, the birds began to build nests on utility poles, prompting utility workers to get rid of the nests. Now, thanks to a ban on DDT and the efforts of volunteers who construct nesting platforms, ospreys are making a comeback.

Snug as a Bug: Orphaned kangaroos and wallabies are quite common in Australia because the mothers don't always make it across the highways. Tailor-made by a conservation group, soft, warm "Joey bags" help the orphaned babies feel safe until they are old enough to face the world on their own.

Egg-o-centric: Because white-naped cranes are seriously endangered, bird experts tried to hatch eggs from captive cranes in incubators. When the project failed, Fred Koontz of the New York Zoological Society came up with a biotelemetric egg—a plastic Easter egg fitted with a battery-operated transmitter—to study nesting practices in the wild. An "eggs-traordinary" success, the egg recorded such things as temperature, humidity, and the number of times it was turned over by the mother bird. The result? Vital information that may increase the ability to hatch eggs laid in captivity.

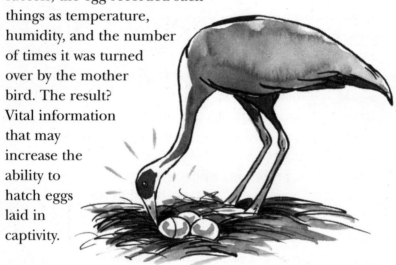

Good News: Scientists thought that the black-footed ferret, once common on the prairie, was extinct. Then in 1981, a small group was discovered on a Wyoming ranch. After a captive breeding program at the Wyoming Zoo, about 200 ferrets were reintroduced to their natural habitat. Several litters have been born in the wild, and scientists are hopeful that this species will soon be off the endangered list.

Toad-ally Alarming:

Scientists concerned about Earth's environment are taking their cues from frogs and toads. Because they drink and breathe through their skin, these animals are very vulnerable to pesticides, fertilizers,

and other pollutants that can eventually hurt people as well. Recently, frogs and toads around the world have begun to disappear. Many others are born with deformities. Luckily, scientists are on the case. They know that solving the mystery of the disappearing frogs and toads will solve some problems for people as well.

Chips Ahoy! Microcomputer technology has become so advanced that tiny birds and toads can be fitted with mini transmitters so biologists can track them by satellite instead of on foot. Scientists think it won't be long now before the equipment will be light enough to attach to a bee!

Creature Feature

For the first time ever recorded, a pair of red-tailed hawks has been observed nesting on . . .

a. a tall building on New York City's Fifth Avenue.
b. the Golden Gate Bridge in California.
c. the Eiffel Tower in Paris.
d. St. Peter's Basilica in Rome.

Fish-eye Lens:

Marine biologist Greg Marshall was deep-sea diving when he saw a shark swim by with a smaller fish attached to it by its suction-cuplike lips. Marshall, a photographer for the National Geographic Society, had a flash of inspiration. "What if I substituted a video camera for the shark-sucker?" So Marshall invented the Crittercam. First designed to get a shark's-eye view of the sea, the Crittercam has since been attached to a variety of other sea creatures, many of them endangered. The Hawaiian monk seal has already benefited. Crittercam videos showed scientists that these animals hunt for food a lot deeper and farther away in the ocean than they had thought. Now the monk seals' waters are protected and their future looks a lot rosier.

Creature Feature

In 2001, an ultralight airplane led a flock of rare young birds from Wisconsin to Florida, where they spent the winter, then successfully flew back on their own. What is this endangered species?

a. Brown pelicans
b. Blue-footed boobies
c. Passenger pigeons
d. Whooping cranes

Scientists have proven that animals in the wild know certain remedies to keep themselves healthy. Which one of these animal survival stories is a sham?

a. Generations of elephants in Kenya have mined special caves near a volcano to get at soft rock that is particularly high in vitamins and minerals.

Believe It!   **Not!**

b. Mosquitoes will not suck the blood of people with colds or illnesses.

Believe It!   **Not!**

c. Chimpanzees with gastrointestinal problems have been known to bite clay off of termite mounds to treat their illness.

Believe It!   **Not!**

d. Capuchin monkeys in Costa Rica have been known to rub a type of chili plant on their fur to ward off insects.

Believe It!   **Not!**

BONUS QUESTION—WILDLIFE WONDER

Skunk spray is actually antibacterial in nature. The skunk not only uses it as a defense mechanism, but also sprays its young to keep them free from germs.

Believe It!   **Not!**

5 To the Rescue!

The courage of animals in the face of danger should never be underestimated.

Tree Service: In 1942, Captain Cyril Jones parachuted into the Sumatran jungle. Entangled in the branches of a tree, he was unable to free himself for 12 days. Jones survived with the help of a monkey, who brought him fruit to eat. When Jones did get free, he was soon captured and taken to a prison camp. The little monkey followed, attacking anyone who bullied him. Afraid that his captors would shoot the monkey, Jones shooed it away, probably saving its life.

Creature Feature

The American Rescue Dog Association, located in Seattle, Washington, prefers using this breed of dog in search and rescue operations:

a. collie.
b. Newfoundland.
c. Saint Bernard.
d. German shepherd.

63

Pulling More Than Her Own Weight: One cold winter day, 36-year-old Michael Miller took Sadie, his English setter, out hunting. Suddenly, a third of a mile into the woods, Miller had a heart attack. He called Sadie with a whistle, then fell to the ground. Unable to walk, Miller held onto Sadie's collar—and the 45-pound dog dragged her 180-pound owner, now semiconscious, all the way back home.

Miller's wife called for an ambulance, and he was rushed to the hospital for emergency surgery. Without Sadie's help, Miller might never have made it out of the woods.

Pig Tale: The day two burglars forced their way into Rebecca Moyer's home, her 300-pound pet pig was taking a snooze in the kitchen. When Arnold heard his owner's screams, he came to the rescue, chomping on one of the bad guy's legs—and sending both crooks scurrying away in fear.

Creature Feature

Rescue dogs work hard to find people buried in debris caused by earthquakes and other disasters, but if they can't find anyone who's alive, they get depressed. To make them feel better, their handlers might . . .

a. bury another worker and let the dog think it's found a live victim.
b. take it for a walk near a peaceful lake.
c. give it a break and let it play with the other rescue dogs.
d. take it out for a big steak dinner.

Porpoise with a Purpose: From 1790 to 1810, a white porpoise named Hatteras Jack guided every ship in and out of Hatteras Inlet, off the coast of North Carolina, and never lost a single vessel.

Shell Shock:

Candelaria Villanueva was thrown into the sea when the ship she was on sank 600 miles south of Manila. Until she was rescued two days later, she was kept afloat by a giant sea turtle. A smaller turtle bit her whenever her head began to droop into the water.

Kitty Pity: Ginny, a dog owned by Philip Gonzalez, seeks out and rescues stray cats from dumpsters, air-conditioning ducts, and other dangerous places. Sometimes she rescues as many as eight injured cats in a week, and hundreds of cats owe their lives to her. There's even a charity named after this heroic dog, the Ginny Fund, that provides money to help cats find good homes and pay their veterinary bills.

Gorilla Posse: When a poacher kidnapped an infant gorilla from its mother, 60 gorillas banded together to get the baby back. In the middle of the night, they invaded a

little village on the border of what was once Equatorial Africa. Ignoring the gunshots fired by villagers, the gorillas banged angrily on doors and windows. Finally, the village chief learned who the poacher was and ordered him to return the kidnapped baby. Appeased, the posse turned around and headed for the forest, beating their chests and screeching with joy.

Breath Saver: Judi Bayly of Nashua, New Hampshire, has a breathing disorder that requires her to wear an oxygen mask while she's sleeping. One night in 1996, Bayly's mask slipped from her face. Lyric, her Irish setter, sprang into action just as he'd been taught. Unable to rouse Bayly, he ran to the phone, knocked the receiver off the hook, and hit the button for 911 three times. When an EMS worker answered, Lyric barked into the receiver and help was soon on its way. The workers who revived Bayly said that they had arrived just in the nick of time.

Creature Feature

In a museum in Italy, there is a statue dating back to the Roman Empire that depicts . . .

a. a lion rescuing a little girl lost in the forest.
b. two large dogs saving drowning people from the sea.
c. three children riding an elephant.
d. a dog dragging a baby from a burning building.

Tag Team: One cold winter day, Chris Georgiou decided to catch up on some yard work at his trout-fishing farm in Australia. Ziggy, his border collie, kept him company, while Stella, his rottweiler, napped about 60 yards away. When Georgiou stood up to rest his back, he banged his head on the railing around the fishing area, lost his balance, and slipped into the icy water. Georgiou couldn't swim, and his heavy clothes weighed him down. Perhaps Ziggy knew that she was too light to pull him out because she stayed nearby, barking frantically to waken Stella. Within seconds, Stella hurtled into the lake, where Georgiou was able to grab her leg and hold on as she towed him to shallow water.

Attack Cat:

Michael Talbot was awakened from a sound sleep by a crash in the next room. He got up to investigate and found an intruder riffling through his possessions. The armed thief ordered Talbot to go back to bed. Not about to argue, Talbot was leaving when Nicky, his gentle, affectionate cat, bolted into the room, growling and hissing. She hurled herself at the intruder, scratching and biting his face. The thief ran, eager to get away from Nicky as fast as possible.

Creature Feature

A statue of a dog named Balto stands in New York City's Central Park to commemorate Balto's work . . .

a. with the New York City Fire Department.
b. delivering medicine to the sick during one of Alaska's worst blizzards.
c. saving hundreds of lives in the Johnstown flood.
d. locating victims in the debris after the Oklahoma City bombing.

Smoke Detector: When actor Drew Barrymore's house caught on fire in February 2001, she was sound asleep in her bedroom. It's a good thing Flossie, Barrymore's Labrador retriever–chow mix, awakened her in time for her to get out before the fire raged through the house.

No Joke: In his early teens, when psychic Uri Geller was living in Cyprus, one of his favorite pastimes was to explore the caves in the hills above his school. One day, Geller went exploring by himself and got lost deep within the caves. He was cold and wet and nothing looked familiar. Worse still, the batteries in his flashlight were about to run out. Geller knew that two of his classmates had gotten lost in the caves and starved to death. Terrified, he had all but given up hope when he felt two paws on his chest. It was his dog, Joker! Geller had no idea how his dog knew where to find him or that he needed finding. But Joker knew the way out, and that's all that mattered.

School of Hard Knocks: When a school of dolphins began to go berserk in the waters just south of Brisbane, Australia, three surfers didn't know what to make of it. Why were the dolphins suddenly diving under their surfboards and poking at them with their noses? Then 17-year-old Adam Maguire saw a shark charging toward him! He punched it in the head and jumped on his board. But the shark came after him, taking a bite out of his board and his hip and knocking Adam into the water as his friends watched in horror. Suddenly, the dolphins went into a frenzy, beating the water with their tails. The distraction gave Adam just enough time to crawl back on his board and float back to shore on the next wave. Adam was airlifted to a hospital, where doctors performed life-saving surgery.

Creature Feature

Scientists have determined that the genetic makeup of humans is most similar to that of . . .

a. pigs.
b. horses.
c. dolphins.
d. chimpanzees.

Pig Power: Priscilla was as happy as a pig could be, swimming with her owner in a lake near Houston, Texas. Suddenly, she was distracted by the panicked cries of 11-year-old Anthony Melton, who was starting to drown. Priscilla took off in his direction and, when she was close enough, began to nudge him with her snout. The sight of a pig in the water jolted Anthony out of his panic long enough for him to grab Priscilla's harness so she could tow him to shore. In 1995, in honor of her super-porcine efforts as a lifeguard, Priscilla became the first animal to be inducted into the Texas Veterinary Medical Association's Hall of Fame.

Creature Feature

Dolphins protect their babies from predators by . . .

a. beating attackers with their snouts.
b. scaring enemies with high-pitched screeches.
c. beating the water with their tails.
d. hiding their babies in seaweed.

Brain Buster

Heroes come in all different shapes and sizes—some even have tails and fur! Three of these remarkable animal rescue stories are true. Can you find the phony?

a. Binti Jua, a gorilla in the Brookfield Zoo in Chicago, Illinois, rescued a three-year-old boy who fell 18 feet into her enclosure.

Believe It! **Not!**

b. In 1890, a rabbit named Misty followed thieves who had burglarized its owner's house. When the owner returned with the police, Misty led them to the thieves' hideout.

Believe It! **Not!**

c. In 1980, a dog named Woody jumped off an 80-foot cliff into a river to save a woman from drowning. Woody kept her afloat until help arrived.

Believe It! **Not!**

d. Scarlett, a stray cat in Brooklyn, New York, hurried in and out of a burning building over and over again, until she had rescued all five of her kittens.

Believe It! **Not!**

BONUS QUESTION—WILDLIFE WONDER

A dentist in Illinois once saved the life of a fish. The golden puffer's teeth had grown so big that the fish could not eat. The dentist filed down its teeth so that the fish could eat again.

Believe It!   **Not!**

POP QUIZ

Think you know everything about these awesome animals? Well, test your smarts with this final Brain Buster. It's a review of the wild and crazy animal facts collected in this book. Ready to go, Tiger?

1. Which of these hard-to-believe food-gathering stories is truly false?
a. Chimpanzees use tools to poke into termite mounds and scare them out.
b. Sea otters bang abalone shells against a rock balanced on their stomach until the shells break open.
c. Vultures crack open the tough shells of ostrich eggs by dropping rocks on them.
d. It takes a penguin seven years to learn to fish with a seaweed net.

2. One of the following animal stories speaks the truth. The rest are false. Can you spot the unbelievable reality?
a. Matt and Cyndi Goodie own a rather musical Yorkshire terrier named Coquito that barks, in key, along with more than 200 different songs.
b. Professor Irene Pepperberg's African gray parrot knows 100 words and can identify 50 different objects.
c. Brooklyn zoologist Craig Morris has trained a team of seals to understand vocal commands. Strangely, the seals only respond to the words when they are sung.
d. Ten-year-old Julie Shermak taught her pet mongoose, Sweetie, to say, "Rock on!"

3. Elephants communicate across long distances by . . .

a. stomping on the ground.

b. sending certain birds to act as messengers.

c. bellowing into trees.

d. sending plant leaves down rivers.

4. Male black-capped chickadees have singing contests to decide who gets to mate with the most females.

Believe It!   Not!

5. Juan Solis of Bolivia, who was blind, was guided by a . . .

a. tortoise.

b. goat.

c. coyote.

d. cat.

6. During World War II, the United States used what kind of bird to deliver secret messages?

a. Sparrow

b. Eagle

c. Turkey

d. Pigeon

7. A fox and a hound *can* be friends! And at the Belstone Hunt in England, such an unlikely pair exists.

Believe It!   Not!

8. Bill, a Jack Russell terrier, helps Ben, another Jack Russell terrier, get around because Ben can't . . .

a. bark.

b. see.

c. hear.

d. smell.

9. Which of these amazing lost-and-found stories is true?

a. Three siblings from California were surfing in Hawaii when a current took their boards far out to sea. A school of dolphins escorted the unharmed teens to shore—right back to the hotel where they were staying.

b. English Private James Brown's dog, Prince, found his master in France during World War II. Apparently, the dog boarded a ship carrying soldiers wearing uniforms like Private Brown's.

c. Stephanie Silvs, an actress from Buffalo, New York, set out on a cross-country tour after leaving her dog, Daisy, with friends. But when the tour ended in Orlando, Florida, there was Daisy, waiting at Silvs's hotel!

d. Italian veterinarian Alexis Fermanis was hiking on a mountain trail when she fell off a cliff. She was knocked unconscious and woke up with amnesia. Luckily, when one of her patients, a clever Labrador retriever, found Fermanis in the hospital, she regained her memory completely.

10. What kind of animal was best man at Terry Lee Griffith's wedding in Stanton, Delaware?

a. A dog
b. A monkey
c. A horse
d. A parrot

11. The tropical rain forests that contain the greatest percentage of the world's animal species are disappearing at a rate of . . .

a. 10 acres per minute.
b. 20 acres per minute.
c. 40 acres per minute.
d. 50 acres per minute.

12. Which zany zoo story is totally untrue?

a. Diablo, an unhappy warthog in Texas, was cheered up when turnips and sweet potatoes were buried in his pen.

b. A polar bear named Gus found a cure for boredom when his zoo pool was turned into a Jacuzzi.

c. Nikki, a Siberian tiger, was scared when the trout in her pool started jumping.

d. A monkey named Max loved the scooters that kids rode outside his cage. When scooters were banned, Max got so depressed, his handlers bought him one of his own!

13. Frogs are very vulnerable to pollution because . . .

a. they drink and breathe through their skin.

b. the flies they eat are carriers.

c. they are attracted to polluted swamps.

d. their eyes are always open.

14. Candelaria Villanueva was thrown into the sea, but kept afloat for two days by a pig.

Believe It!   Not!

15. Which one of these four animal alarm stories is not alarming at all (because it's not true!)?

a. Rebecca Moyer's pet pig chomped on the leg of a burglar, sending the two thieves running away.

b. When Anat Leonard fell asleep with a candle burning by her bedside, her goldfish jumped out of its bowl and flung itself onto Leonard's pillow. Leonard woke up, put the fish back in its bowl, and blew out the candle.

c. Michael Talbot's cat, Nicky, hurled herself at a late-night burglar, causing him to run away.

d. Drew Barrymore's pet dog woke her up when her house caught fire.

Answer Key

Chapter 1
Smarter Than You Think!
Page 5:   **c.** frightened.

Page 6:   **a.** sponges.

Page 9:   **c.** is infected with *Toxoplasma gondii.*

Page 11:   **a.** when they are shown photos.

Page 12:   **b.** watching the flight patterns of other birds.

Page 15:   **a.** squawked "boat."

Page 17:   **d.** understand fractions.

Page 18:   **d.** build castles with Lego toys.

Page 20:   **a.** an orangutan that regularly dismantles his cage.

Brain Buster: d. is false.

Bonus Question: Believe It!

Chapter 2
Can-do Critters
Page 23:   **a.** 300-pound ostrich.

Page 25:   **a.** an ordained minister.

Page 27:   **c.** camels pulling a car with no engine.

Page 29:   **a.** Bear Field, because a trained bear was used to clear the construction site.

Page 30:   **b.** trim the White House lawn.

Page 32:   **d.** pigs in pantaloons dancing to bagpipes.

Brain Buster: c. is false.

Bonus Question: Believe It!

Chapter 3
Helping Hands & Friendly Paws
Page 35:   **b.** 25 chicks.

Page 36:   **d.** python.

Page 39:   **d.** skin cancer.

Page 40:   **a.** pushing her into a chair.

Page 43:   **d.** reserve a cat to keep them company for the night.

Page 44:   **a.** lower blood pressure.

Page 46:   **b.** labradoodle (Labrador retriever and poodle).

Page 48:   **c.** emu.

Brain Buster: a. is false.

Bonus Question: Not!

Chapter 4
Good Breeding
Page 51:   **b.** Siberian tigers

Page 53:   **a.** European bison

Page 54:   **d.** eight months.

Page 56:   **d.** 30,000.

Page 59:   **a.** a tall building on New York City's Fifth Avenue.

Page 60:   **d.** Whooping cranes

Brain Buster: b. is false.

Bonus Question: Not!

Chapter 5
To the Rescue

Page 63:   **d.** German shepherd.

Page 64:   **a.** bury another worker and let the dog think it's found a live victim.

Page 67:   **b.** two large dogs saving drowning people from the sea.

Page 69:   **b.** delivering medicine to the sick during one of Alaska's worst blizzards.

Page 71:   **c.** dolphins.

Page 72:   **c.** beating the water with their tails.

Brain Buster: **b.** is false.

Bonus Question: Believe It!

Pop Quiz

1.   **d.**
2.   **b.**
3.   **a.**
4.   **Believe It!**
5.   **a.**
6.   **d.**
7.   **Believe It!**
8.   **b.**
9.   **b.**
10.   **c.**
11.   **d.**
12.   **d.**
13.   **a.**
14.   **Not!**
15.   **b.**

What's Your Ripley's Rank?

Ripley's Scorecard

Congratulations! You've done a whale of a job spotting fictions among all these amazing animal facts! Now it's time to tally up your answers and get your Ripley's rating. Are you **Catnapping on the Job**? Or are you **Like a Fish in the Sea**? Add up your scores to find out.

Here's the scoring breakdown. Give yourself:

★ **10 points** for every **Creature Feature** you got right;

★ **20 points** for every fiction you spotted in the **Ripley's Brain Busters**;

★ **10 points** every time you solved a **Wildlife Wonder**;

★ and **5 points** for every **Pop Quiz** question you answered correctly.

Here's a tally sheet:

Number of **Creature Feature**
questions answered correctly: _____ x 10 = _____
Number of **Ripley's Brain Buster**
fictions spotted: _____ x 20 = _____
Number of **Wildlife Wonder**
questions solved: _____ x 10 = _____
Number of **Pop Quiz** questions
answered correctly: _____ x 5 = _____

Total the right column for your final score: _____

0–100
Catnapping on the Job?

Rise and shine and welcome to the world of Robert Ripley! There are amazing, unbelievable facts all around you, and it's time you started taking notice. The animal kingdom is just one place to find extraordinary happenings. Inventors, bugs, history—there are weird and wacky elements to just about every subject in the world—but only if you decide to look!

101–250
Doggone Amazing!

You are pawing your way along, learning all about the amazing animal kingdom. Now we just have to better acquaint you with Robert Ripley's collection of all things bizarre and unusual. That way you'll be able to tell the unbelievable from the untrue—a very difficult distinction in Ripley's world!

251–400
No Monkey Business

You are getting serious about the wild and wacky animal kingdom. No slipping any funky fictions by you—you've got a great grasp of the unbelievable! How did you learn so much about the unusual? You must be a Ripley's regular. Which means you know that there are all kinds of bizarre stories out there!

401–575
Like a Fish in the Sea

They say that elephants never forget, and neither do you! You have an amazing knack for wacky animal facts. And you can easily tell when someone is just monkeying around with fake answers! You are at the top of the Ripley's food chain—and for good reason!

Believe It!®

Photo Credits

Ripley Entertainment Inc. and the editors of this book wish to thank the following photographers, agents, and other individuals for permission to use and reprint the following photographs in this book. Any photographs included in this book that are not acknowledged below are property of the Ripley Archives. Great effort has been made to obtain permission from the owners of all materials included in this book. Any errors that may have been made are unintentional and will gladly be corrected in future printings if notice is sent to Ripley Entertainment Inc., 5728 Major Boulevard, Orlando, Florida 32819.

Black & White Photos

7   Sea Otter; 15 Elephant; 18 Black-capped Chickadee; 53 Baby Condor and Hand Puppet; 59 Frog/U.S. Fish and Wildlife Service

12 Azy/Jessie Cohen/National Zoological Park/Smithsonian Institution

17 Lions Attacking Wildebeest/Al Robinson

24 Ping/Courtesy Michele Brown

26 Seeing Eye Dog/KRT

28 Dan Shaw and Cuddles/Courtesy Janet Burleson

30 Capuchin Monkey/PhotoDisc

37 Linus and Angel/Mary Packard

39 Clever Hans/Copyright Unknown/From the Book *Clever Hans* by Oskar Pfungst/New York, Henry Holt and Company, 1911

40 Brian Revheim and Arthur/Megan Revheim

42 Racing Pigeon/Courtesy Paul Walsh/ http://walshloft.com

44 The Rauschers and Cody; 48 Carol Piccione and Shadow/© 2002 Newsday, Inc./Reprinted with Permission

45 Dolphins/Hemera

47 Dog Wearing Bowlingual/Takara Co., Ltd.

52 Mike Archer and Tasmanian Tiger; 55 Penguin Rescue/Reuters Photo Archive

64 Michael Miller and Sadie/PR Newswire Photo Service

70 Drew Barrymore/Zuma Press

Color Insert

Flea Circus/Courtesy Eddie Diijon

Tillamook Cheddar and Painting/Courtesy Bowman Hastie

Sunset Sam/Courtesy Clearwater Marine Aquarium, Clearwater, Florida

Sunset on the Adriatic Sea by Boronali/ Copyright Unknown

Thai Elephant Orchestra/Neil Budzinski

Aurthur/Dr. Bhagavan Antle/T.I.G.E.R.S. (The Institute of Greatly Endangered and Rare Species), Myrtle Beach, South Carolina/www.tigers-animal-actors.com

Background Palette; Ferret; Background Ferret/PhotoDisc

Giraffes; Baby Kangaroo/Ablestock

Gorilla/Konrad Wothe/Minden Pictures

Blue Whale/ Phillip Colla Photography/ www.OceanLight.com

Cheetahs/CORBIS

Three-toed Sloth/Gerry Ellis/Minden Pictures

Pygmy Mouse Lemur/© Karl Lehmann

Infant and Bullet/© 2002 Newsday, Inc./Reprinted with Permission

Joleen Walderbach and Shelby/PR Newswire Photo Service

Binti Jua/KRT

Ferret/PhotoDisc

Bomb Dog/Getty Images

RIPLEY's
Believe It or Not!®

The weird...the wacky...the bizarre.
Collect them all!

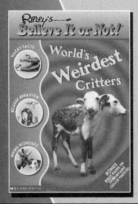